THE TRINITY

An Introduction

Ronnie Aitchison

ISBN 9798884625914

CONTENTS

INTRODUCTION

Shortly after I retired I decided to read all I could on the theology of the Trinity, this took more than a couple of years, not full time, but when I could. By the time I ended the research I had an A4 copier box full of notes and references. My intention had been to write MY book on the Trinity.

After several false starts and several years I came to the realisation that my problem was that I did not actually have anything new to say on the subject.

This book is my way of using all that research in a way that suits my abilities.

What I hope this essay6 provides is an introduction to the theology of the Trinity for the lay person and the interested explorer.

I have tried to use as few technical terms as possible and where used I have tried to explain them in a plain language form.

The Trinity is spoken of often in the Church, sometimes just in its individual terms, but if churches are not to simply subside into Unitarianism we need to understand what we mean by the Trinity which allows us to own it.

Ronnie Aitchison

CHAPTER ONE

As an active minister I was sometimes told "there are just as many good Christians outside the church as in it." By which the person speaking meant "good people", but equated that concept with Christianity.

This is, of course, untrue. It is a total misconception of the term Christian. That there are good people of all faiths and none is an undoubted truth, but this is not the criteria for judging someone's Christianity. When we claim that title, for ourselves, or someone else, we are making a statement regarding faith. It is this that is so often misunderstood. Whilst there are many Christian denominations there are certain central tenets common to them all.

At Christmas we celebrate the coming into the world of the Christ child, the incarnation. Too often this event gets swamped, even amongst adult worshippers, by a sentimental story about a helpless baby and a single mother struggling against the odds. This is not the story told in the bible. In Matthew 1:22 we read all this took place to fulfil what the Lord had said through the prophet: "The virgin will be with child and will give birth to a son, and they will call him Immanuel" – which means "God with us." Luke offers a similar announcement when the angel tells Mary. "You will be with child and give birth to a son, and you are to give him the name Jesus. He will be great and will be called the Son of the Most High. The Lord will give him the throne of David, and he will reign over the house of Jacob for ever; his kingdom will never end.[1] Neither of these statements is about humble birth or weakness. And Mary has been signally honoured by God.

---

[1] Luke Chapter 1 verses 35-37 NIV.

Throughout the two millennia since, the Church has proclaimed this event as the incarnation. As John describes it in his opening chapter, "the Word was made flesh and made his dwelling among us". What John suggests and what the Church claims is that God took on human form and came to live here on earth as witness to the totality of his love for us and to offer us an opportunity to relate to our God in a more intimate way than had previously been possible. It is engaging with this event which allows one to call oneself a Christian. If one does, then we commit to living a Christian life and that is where the concept of a Christian as a good person resides. But it is through the faith commitment that we become Christians and it is that faith which separates us from non-believers and those of other faiths.

Why does it matter what you believe?

If you want to lead a good life, there are many avenues to that goal; in fact there are many ways of defining the goal. It is not for me to suggest that your path is not a good one. Christianity is more than an attempt to lead a good life. It offers a relationship with God, and a promise of life eternal. Right away, you can see that these statements will cause many people to pause, particularly in this time and in the world as it is. Religious faith does cause people problems today as they consider the scientific world and the challenge of moving beyond the unknown, nonetheless, that is what religions call upon their followers to do. It is in this context that Christian goodness is consequential; it is a result of our faith.

There are three monotheistic faiths in the Abrahamic line, Judaism, Christianity, and Islam. Each of these claims to be the one true path. Owing to the history of their foundation, Islam recognises the prophets of the other two and Jesus as a major prophet, Christianity recognises the prophets of Judaism and all its writings as an essential ingredient of its story but sees Islam as a later aberration, yet all claim a common history at their root. The antagonism that exists between these faiths is to some degree understandable as each claim to possess the ONLY truth. Within these faiths there are differences and sometimes claims of heresy against groups who hold some part of the story differently. This is not an essay in comparative religion so the workings of Judaism and Islam will be left to others to consider, but Christianity has had divisions since its very beginnings and for periods of its history deep antagonism between denominations or sects. Part of its early history was the attempts to define what were the core, essential understandings that made Christian faith a unity. These questions were argued and written about and discussed, sometimes acrimoniously, sometimes in deep intellectual argument for much of the early life of the Church. This led to the great Councils of the 4th century and beyond which attempted to create a unified theology and in particular an acceptable understanding of the person of Jesus Christ. Beginning with the First Council of Nicea in AD 325 such "ecumenical" Councils took place up to the Second Council of Nicea in 787. Seven in total, and, although not all present day churches accept all seven of these as authoritative, by tradition they are "ecumenical". This terminology and the understanding of a large part of Christianity regarding the Councils strongly suggests that the catholicity of the church was defined best by the lower case understanding, ie liberal, rather than universal as inferred by the use of the capital. I do not mean to suggest a fractured Church, rather a group of churches growing in different parts of the early world, in different cultures. These different contexts, and often the way this had affected their ecclesiology had brought about alternative ways of operating and of understanding the idea of church. Alongside this were the distinctive cultural philosophical styles that affected the way ideas were expressed and language could be understood. Culture is rarely static, but it is a powerful influence on behaviour, understanding and societal acceptance at any time. Similarly, although most educated Christians in the early centuries spoke or understood Greek this did not mean that they thought as Greeks did and such differences created subtle nuances in the means of describing what they all believed.

In the west we tend to think that the Reformation brought about the largest schism in the Christian church, but that is because we usually ignore the Orthodox Church which finally separated in the 11th century and we take little note of the Coptic Church which dates from 190AD or groups such as the Church in Ethiopia and the Syriac Church which claim a very early foundation.

The most difficult question!

Almost from the beginning of the Christian Church the most controversial question was "who was Jesus?". This would seem to be a strange problem for a church apparently based on the beliefs born out of the preaching of Paul, the Apostles and the witness of the Jerusalem Church, but any reading of Paul's letters would show that there were other teachers in the countries spreading out from the founding source. Many of whom it seems had picked up some knowledge or ideas without being part of the root source. To a greater or larger extent this sort of problem has bedevilled Christianity throughout its history. During the early centuries there were debates and plain arguments about the basic question, the divinity of Jesus. Even when this was settled within the core churches many thinkers struggled with the "how" can this be?

It was in the crucible of this struggle that the Trinity as answer was born. It is often stated that the Trinity does not exist in the bible. This is true linguistically, but in both old and new testaments there are statements which require an understanding of God as acting through different mediums. God's Spirit hovers over the waters during creation and his creation is enacted by his Word. In Mark, Jesus rebukes the wind and the storm dies down. This action is placed in the clear context of divine power over nature. To John who describes Jesus as the Word. Each of these have agency, the Spirit in the beginning, the Word in creation and Jesus in his command of the elements.

The early Church Fathers had no doubt that Jesus was the Son of God, but they had to answer those who doubted. In promulgating these answers they developed the concept of the Trinity. Language was at the core of their explanations, a particular expression of ideas. It is in the loose use of language in modern times that the Trinity becomes vague. The creeds speak of one God: Father, Son and Holy Spirit. Sometimes today there is a tendency to conflate God and Father and use the terms interchangeably. This misuse tends to blur the understanding of what is meant.

In a paper by Loraine Boettner published on the internet by caledonianfire.org, she writes "The doctrine of the Trinity *cannot* (my italics) lead to Tritheism; for while there are three Persons in the Godhead, there is but one substance or essence, and therefore one God. It is rather a case of the one life substance, Deity, existing consciously as three Persons." If only that *cannot* were matched by experience of encounters with other equally confident writers. It is not that all writers in whom one might encounter an apparent tritheism present this intentionally, it is more often a case that there seems to be at least three people present in their description.

The lifebelt comes from Karl Rahner. It is a rather strange lifebelt, but it offers the possibility that certainty can be superseded by a faithful quest. What Rahner offers is that the Trinity "is an absolute mystery which we do not understand even after it has been revealed."[2] Each generation of writers and theologians has produced new insights or interpretations of old insights which can be accepted as answers, but not definitions. A mystery remains a mystery until it is solved. There are a long line of theologians who have tried to shed light on this mystery, few who claim that it is solved. The creeds do not claim to solve the mystery, but to state the Church's understanding of it. To claim that these things are true still leaves the question of how can they be true? It also does not tell us if these things are the whole truth. We are left with the quest.

[2]Rahner, Karl, *The Trinity*, p 50.

CHAPTER TWO

In the vast tapestry of Christian theology, few doctrines are as profound and central as that of the Trinity. For beginners stepping into the theological terrain, the Trinity might initially seem like a complex and mysterious concept. However, it is this very mystery that has captivated the minds of theologians for centuries and serves as the cornerstone of Christian understanding of God.

The Quest

Imagine embarking on a journey to comprehend the nature of God. This quest has engaged the minds of theologians, scholars, and believers throughout the ages. The Trinity, though challenging to grasp fully, is a foundational aspect of Christian faith. It invites us to explore the inner workings of the Divine, a mystery that unfolds across the pages of Scripture and the annals of Christian tradition.

A journey which is only about arriving, is generally tedious. Perhaps tiring and is, in many ways, lost time and effort. There is another kind of journey, that sort of travel which is about seeing, hearing and exploring new places and new people. A quest should really be like the latter form of journey. What is worthwhile is what is discovered along the way. It was in this context that I set out to explore the doctrine of the Trinity. To do this involved a great deal of reading in several libraries, exploring the work of theologians throughout the life of the Church. To be honest, while I read many of the early writers, in the end I concentrated on the theologians of the nineteenth and twentieth century, which was still a vast collection of works and the accruing of a collection of notes which filled an A4 copier paper box.

I don't intend to offer all that information, my purpose here is to offer a condensed and, hopefully, understandable, telling of the Trinity that is at the heart of our Christian faith.

The Divine Community

At its core, the Trinity reveals a God who exists in community. Unlike any other concept of deity, the Christian understanding of God is not a solitary figure dwelling in isolated splendour. Instead, we encounter a divine community—the Father, the Son (Jesus Christ), and the Holy Spirit—existing eternally in perfect unity and love.

Theologians throughout the history of the church have described the Trinity through two separate but connected visions of the Trinity. One of these is termed "the immanent Trinity". This term focuses on God in Himself, apart from His interactions with the world. It asks us to look into the eternal relationships within the Godhead. Here, we encounter a profound unity and equality among the three persons, a dance of love that theologians often describe as perichoresis, a mutual indwelling. We will come to that term again later.

The second way of looking at the Trinity is called the Economic Trinity, in this we see God in action, the roles each person of the Trinity plays in the story of creation, redemption, and sanctification. The Father initiates, the Son redeems, and the Holy Spirit empowers. This dynamic interplay reveals a God who is intimately involved in the unfolding drama of human history. These terms are not universally accepted but they describe the understanding of a God of action.

Another way of describing the two terms would be that the immanent Trinity describes the relationships between the three persons as a shared love which is at the centre of the being of God. For many theologians to say God is Love encompasses this concept.

The economic Trinity can be described as God's activities in relation to the world. One of the problems with some of the descriptions used is that to describe each person of the Trinity as having an individual role ie, creator, redeemer, empowerer tends to be seen as a form of modalism, by which is meant that we are defining the persons by what they do which inevitably means we see them as three people.

A simplified way to look at these to ideas would:

Immanent describes the internal relationships of God

And economic describes the external roles in relation to the world, particularly in the story of salvation.

What Do We Believe?

Norman Wallwork in his short work on the Trinity[3] was concerned that in reality most Methodists (and most Christians) had no understanding of the Trinity, and of more concern to him had no relationship with it in their worship.

Karl Rahner points the finger very clearly at this problem when he states that "the Christian's idea of the incarnation would not have to change at all if there were no Trinity." It is not that Rahner questions the average Christian's belief per se, but that he suggests that the detail is hazy and that accepted theology since the time of Augustine has not really helped to clarify the detail such as to help interested Christian to speak of the Trinity coherently and with one voice.

---

[3] The Forgotten Trinity in Contemporary Methodism, Norman Wallwork, 2004, Methodist Sacramental fellowship

It could be assumed that, since most Christians have confessed the creed at some time in liturgy or at entry into the Church, they would believe what they have professed. Discussions with groups from a variety of congregations suggest otherwise. Even those in ministry cannot, confidently, be counted as those who accept all that the creeds say without question.

Theologians, too, have offered differences of interpretation, if a more certain belief. Of course the whole purpose of the creeds was to set up a boundary between what was acceptable theology and what was not. The Church was setting standards for believing and excluding beliefs which did not fit the primary understanding or which offered explanations that could lead away from the central tenet of faith of the young church, that Jesus Christ was God made flesh.

Creating a framework in which Jesus was God and which also explained why this same Jesus could speak of his Father in heaven, could pray to this Father and speak of being alongside Him was always going to be a difficult balancing act, verging on a conjuring trick. It was not easily arrived at and agreement was a long struggle. One of the insuperable difficulties has been the division in expression, and therefore understanding, between the churches of the East and the West. For the "average Christian" the subtleties of the argument as to whether the Holy Spirit proceeds from the Father and the Son, as the Western Church says, or from the Father through the Son, as the Eastern Church has it, are incomprehensible and probably even seem irrelevant. Yet from the very beginning of the discussion much has rested on such fine understandings, to a great degree a matter of semantics.

But we don't believe the semantics, it is not the definitions which are at the heart of our belief. Christians must start from a position of faith. Without a faith, there is no need for words to explain what we believe. The creeds and our doctrinal statements are intended to help us understand the mystery that is faith. Here is the core of the matter. Christians believe in God, most Christians believe in Jesus as the Son of God and therefore divine, nearly all Christians seem to accept the existence of the Holy Spirit putting these three concepts together is something far less frequently done. So "we believe in the Trinity" can, all too often, produce a slightly vague response and a degree of reluctance to discuss the concept. The reaction of preachers to Trinity Sunday is an example of this difficulty.

There is probably little point in introducing the concerns of those church goers or adherents who are struggling with the idea of Jesus as divine and who are more comfortable with the "good man" image when discussing the complexities of the Trinity, so I will try to speak only to the concerns of Christians for whom the incarnation is a reality within their Christian faith. Within these strictures we are still left with a great variety of views and a tremendous width of understandings. Leonard Boff[4] quotes Kant's view of the doctrine of the Trinity: "The doctrine of the Trinity provides nothing, absolutely nothing, of practical value, even if one claims to understand it; still less when one is convinced that it far surpasses our understanding. It costs the student nothing to accept that we adore three or ten persons in the divinity. One is the same as the other to him, since he has no concept of God in different persons(hypostases). Furthermore, this distinction offers absolutely no guidance for his conduct." This brings Boff to the view that the Trinity, for most people, has become a problem in logic and has ceased to be the mystery of our salvation. I think that Boff may be too pessimistic

---

[4] Boff, *Trinity and Society*, p19.

. It is true that reading widely amongst the theological and philosophical works on the Trinity it would be possible to see things in this way. As I have said, it is often presented as though it were a problem in semantics or, as Boff suggests, logic.

Nonetheless the Roman church and the Orthodox in different ways start from the view that the Trinity is, in fact, a divine mystery. Despite that understanding their theologians find themselves with a need to try to understand the mystery and then to explain it. Protestant and Reformed theologians have been more inclined towards the logical. Karl Barth's view that we must gain our understanding of God from his revelation has led to an analytical approach to doctrine based on an examination of salvation history as we know it. These two approaches offer differing tools to explain and to understand what is meant when we speak of three persons, one God.

These two basic approaches have one thing in common, "we believe". The difference, you could say, is a matter of style, or emphasis but that would not be the whole truth. At the simplest level, the revelation approach is easy to grasp, but the moment you attempt to explain or describe what you understand the more likely you are to fall into one or other of the classic heresies almost every attempt to provide a simple illustration of the Trinity slides inadvertently into some level of modalism or tritheism (more of which later). To take the path of mystery allows those who do not feel the need to possess a rational explanation for their belief to sidestep the question with an acceptance that the divine is beyond our capacity to understand or to grasp completely.

Does It Matter?

If we proclaim ourselves as Christians what we believe matters a great deal. Some years ago a group of young people from a Christian church was invited to go to a mosque and engage in discussion with a similar group of young Muslims. What embarrassed the leader was that the Muslim youngsters not only knew the stories and beliefs of their own faith, but they were better versed in those of Christianity than the church group. When it came to arguing doctrine the young Christians were outclassed. The Trinity was, of course, a particular area of attack by the Muslim group who suggested that Christianity had three Gods. The Christian young people were largely unable to explain their "belief" in this matter, and found themselves puzzled as to how to explain this God in whom they were supposed to believe. They were all monotheists, but not clearly Trinitarian monotheists.

In much the same way I have found that bible studies on the Trinity with groups who have been brought up in the church, who have felt themselves to be comfortable in their Christian faith, have often become a struggle, sometimes arousing tensions which were not obvious previously. On a couple of occasions these have culminated in people who were key persons in their congregation simply rejecting the divinity of Jesus, "because it made no sense".

These experiences suggest that what we believe matters, but even more that what we teach is taught in such a way as to engage the hearer in a positive response. Ultimately it doesn't matter whether what they engage with is the mystery or the intellectual challenge of the doctrine. What does matter is that the people who receive this teaching should be able to own it and fit it into the wholeness of their faith. It seems to me that this is an enormous challenge for those of us called to be preachers and teachers in Christ's church.

CHAPTER THREE

Are We Trinitarian?

A 2002 lecture for the Methodist Sacramental Fellowship was entitled "WHAT EVER HAPPENED TO THE FATHER? The Jesus Heresy in Modern Worship"[5]. It's main thrust was against those groups in the church today who focus all their worship activity on the person and name of Jesus - to the exclusion of the Father. The writer particularly pointed to the preponderance of Jesus language in the worship songs favoured by many of the more charismatic church groups. Of course it would probably be equally possible to demonstrate that many of the same groups were much inclined to the invocation of the Holy Spirit. These tendencies are real. They may appear in the form of a particular focus on the worship of Jesus, or of the worship of the Holy Spirit, or both. What is common is that the Father can seem to almost vanish.

It would be equally possible to find congregations where the Holy Spirit is hardly mentioned and if any such allusion is outside of a formal part of the liturgy that reference would be more likely to induce embarrassment than awaken interest. I was recently at a service where the minister set out on what was intended to be a "Trinitarian" explanation of John 14 which was going well until she started to talk about "the spirit of Jesus" dwelling in us. This formula infers that it is Jesus who dwells in us as spirit, not the Holy Spirit which John intended. Which is clear if you read verse 25.

Father too has its problems in today's society. There is a considerable movement towards banishing its use as a term for God as many people now have a negative view of fathers to a greater or lesser degree. There is also the problem for the feminist Christian that she will feel excluded by the language.

---

[5] WHAT EVER HAPPENED TO THE FATHER? The Jesus Heresy in Modern Worship, Susan J. White, The Methodist Sacramental Fellowship Lecture 2002, Wolverhampton.

Within our churches today it may be that we could find a significant number of people who see the Holy Spirit as only attractive to the superstitious and emotional, Father as an unacceptable term for a loving God and Jesus as a prophet or just a healer. What is of particular concern in this situation is that we are dealing with the basic ideas and concepts which make up our faith. When earlier I spoke of the semantics which surround the doctrine of the Trinity I was acknowledging the difficulty of finding words which express the concepts which are integral to the divine mystery. These latest developments have taken our concerns back to the second century struggles, before the church was able to offer a unified statement of faith with a coherent understanding of the Christ event and the Gospel message.I would suggest that this problem has always existed; that the "average Christian" in almost every age has been as likely to be polytheist as Trinitarian, or at best monotheist. Certainly in modern times, and I suspect through most ages, the polytheism would be involuntary, a simple problem of practical application rather than a conscious belief in several gods. Most of what we say about our faith and its source is said in simple language. Technical language, sometimes referred to as "churchy jargon", is said to be unhelpful for worshippers and in particular for those coming into church from a non-church background. This promotion of simple language has many advantages, but it also brings with it pitfalls. From the time of the Reformation, it has been axiomatic that the bible should be available in the vernacular so that the ordinary worshipper could become familiar with the truths of their faith. This attempt to make available to all Christians the Word of God meant that concepts, such as the Trinity, which had been the domain of the theologian had to be taught as part of that inclusion. The early church fathers had struggled to find words which could express exactly what they meant when defining this doctrine, Augustine[6] took twenty-eight years to write his work and was still not satisfied with it.

---

[6] Augustine of Hippo, On The Trinity

Translating it into Latin brought further problems of agreement and in today's modern languages we have an equally huge problem. For the early fathers the problem was confined to a limited number of theologians. Even in the Greek speaking world few people could read and even fewer would have access to the texts around which there was an argument. In the English speaking parts of the world, almost every Christian will be able to read and most will be asked to confess a faith in a form of words which, treated simply, present real difficulties of understanding. We ask people to worship God the Father through Jesus his Son. Technically we are speaking of two "persons", but for all practical purposes we have two "people" and it is in this language and the usage that I see people's polytheism. Rahner said that Christians were "in their practical life, mere monotheists"[7] and in many ways this would be the reality for many people. The polytheism is in their connection to the ideas as expressed. By this I mean that people tend to behave monotheistically, but to think and speak polytheistically. For many people neither of these situations is a problem, they operate their faith life at a non-complex level having accepted a belief system which could raise many difficult questions, they are not interested in asking these questions. Throughout the history of the church there have been those who have taken the statements of the church and attempted to offer an understanding which can be received by a wider audience, or agreed by their contemporary peers. The doctrine of the Trinity has presented more problems to such writers than almost anything else. Today our church congregations have a high proportion of people who are not professional theologians, but who are used to thinking for themselves and making decisions based on their own reading of information presented. For such people what is offered in the case of the Trinity raises more questions than it does acceptable answers. Some simply slip seamlessly into a form of

---

[7]Rahner, *The Trinity*, p10.

Unitarianism[8], others crash into a logical hurdle and may not return to the race.

The Trinity is very much in fashion at the present time, in particular the concept of the social trinity has brought new insights into this area, although these new ways of looking at the Trinity can lead one to see a multiplicity rather than a unity. Feminist writers have also found a positive place for this doctrine but here too there are strange byways. It does not take long in exploring feminist writings before you find at least four persons present in this Trinitarian community. To avoid these difficulties seems to require the concentration of a tightrope walker crossing Niagara Falls, it is necessary to look neither to left nor right, but concentrate on the set path and believe. Perhaps this is the key to the problem, the Trinity is a doctrine propounded to answer "how" questions which only raise their heads when we are not sure of what we say we believe.

---

[8] Unitarians deny the divinity of Jesus. Although this is a simplification today as some "Unitarian" churches are non-religious

CHAPTER FOUR

Why are we a Trinitarian religion - i.e. not monotheistic

Christianity is rooted in Judaism, Jesus and all his immediate followers were Jews, Paul even boasts of his Jewishness as giving him authority. So why has Christianity moved away from that primary Judaistic understanding of one indivisible God? Perhaps that question would be better phrased 'so has Christianity moved away from . . .' For, at core, that is the area where clarity becomes fuzzy at the edges. The other two Abrahamic faiths are absolutely clear that God (Yahweh/Allah) is one and is indivisible. Trinitarian Christianity states that God is Father, Son and Holy Spirit, ONE IN UNITY.

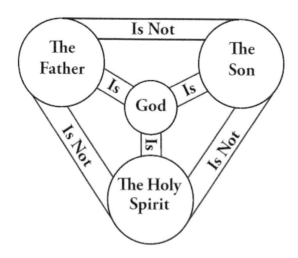

The Early Church

For early Christians the doctrine of the Trinity was an attempt to express the God whom they had encountered. The Trinity is a fact of revelation. We see this expressed in the teaching of the church fathers and the writers of the creeds. They knew God and worshipped him, but they believed that Jesus was the Son of God, the incarnation as expressed in the Gospel of John. Belief was the key point. The Christ Jesus whom Paul declares in his introduction to Romans is not a prophet or a simple human messenger from Yahweh. This is the Son of God, the Lord Jesus Christ a "person" whom Paul has described in terms which elevate him beyond the normal. All that Paul has to say about Jesus places him in this very special position, it is through the activity of Jesus, the risen Lord, that Paul is imbued with the Holy Spirit in Damascus. The early church was not trying to invent God, or even a new religion, it was trying to express, in ways that they could pass on to others, an experience which they had received from the primary sources.

It is likely that if there had been one clear explicable source for the understandings which permeated the first churches there would have been far less need for the Councils or even for the creeds. The world in the first century did not operate such as to make this a real possibility. But what little we actually know of the missionary period suggests that, not only were there a number of different missioners, but they did not all originate in the same source. Our four canonical Gospels demonstrate sufficient variation to create quite different branches of Christian understanding without even allowing for the effect of interpretation and transmission by word of mouth.

It was inevitable that the Churches, once settled and to some extent formalised, should need to agree amongst themselves what it was they intended to convey about this Jesus whom they called Lord and Saviour. What was the salvation of which they spoke, how was it offered and received and how did it affect their relationship with God.

Within the lengthy quest to come to an agreement on these matters awareness must have emerged of this central difficulty: who did they claim Jesus was, and what was his relationship to the God he called Father. In the first two hundred years of questioning it was probably even more difficult to come to a consensus than it is in this post-modern world. Their need for answers which could be owned by all Christians led to the attacks on heresies in this period. A refusal to accept the view of the general was certain to lead to rejection from the community. Perhaps the most telling influence was that of Greek philosophy, as much as anything else, because its practitioners were accustomed to analytical thought and argument. The oriental Jews were accustomed to expressing ideas in symbolic terms and through the use of parabolic[9]

exploration of ideas, the spread of Christianity to the area of influence of Greek logic required a completely new way of expression, the language used became crucial and had to be capable of a very precise meaning.

---

[9] In this sense it infers relation to the parables

In the beginning

Matthew and Luke each have a description of the birth of Jesus which suggests a particular relationship with God. In verses 18-22 of chapter One Matthew tells us how Joseph is instructed by an angel about what is happening with Mary. Not, curiously, a passage which has elicited as much comment as the equivalent Lucan story, yet one which draws attention to the faithfulness and obedience of Joseph. This passage starts with the statement that Mary is with child "through the Holy Spirit", and closes with the declaration that this child will be called Immanuel, which means God with us. The writer brackets the conception story with very powerful inferences about the child and what we should understand about him, although this is expressed in the language forms and concepts of the Jewish world.

Luke starts his Gospel by telling us that what he tells us has been handed down to him from "those who were eyewitnesses and servants of the Word". He then goes on to offer much the same story as Matthew, except that his is focussed on Mary as the centre of the events and the communication. This story is less clear and more ambiguous about the person of the child, but it is none the less a story of an interaction between the creator and his world. Much is made of Luke's use of the guarantee of authenticity in his prologue. In verse two he names the "servants of the word" amongst those guarantors which offer some echoes of the "Word" in the opening verses of John's Gospel.. While we cannot assume that Luke was using "the Word" in the same sense that John did he clearly wants us to understand the birth narrative as something of divine activity.

John opens with an expression of faith rooted firmly in the Jewish tradition and in that understanding of the being of God. There is nothing oblique about John, he makes powerful claims about the person he describes through his opening and the words he puts into the mouth of John the Baptist. In chapter twenty he encapsulates the earlier theological statements about Jesus with Thomas's statement "My Lord and my God."

With these as the starting points from which to explain Christianity to the world the early Church fathers were faced with a problem in offering a reconciliation between the stated belief in one God and the professions of faith in the divinity of Jesus. While the early history of the Church and the struggles with "heresies" demonstrate some of the variety of paths this resolution was to take, the path which culminates in the doctrine of the Trinity is that which interests us at this time.

Since early in the life of the Church, theologians have struggled with this need to explain how God could be one and indivisible and yet be present on earth in the person of Jesus, a man. As a consequence of this struggle they began to reflect on what the Bible said of the Spirit of God and how he/she fitted into this equation.

The Spirit of God

The Old Testament opens with an introduction to the Spirit of God who hovered over the waters and was active in the creation of the universe. The New Testament, as we have it ordered, opens with the activity of the Holy Spirit in the conception of the child who was to become Jesus. Doubtless this is no accident as those who wrote and compiled the New Testament were all influenced by the scriptures which they already had.

Despite this early inclusion of the action of the Holy Spirit as decisive in the incarnation story there was a gentle slide away from a truly positive pneumatology in the church in the west. The BCC Study Commission on Trinitarian Doctrine Today[10] describes on pp27-28 some of the differences which gradually entered the theology of the Western Church as the Spirit more and more often was spoken and written of as the activity of Christ rather than a distinct persona in its own right. This shift in emphasis led quite early to the filioque problem, brought about by the addition made by the Western Church to the original Nicene Creed that 'the Spirit proceeds from the Father *and the Son'*. The Eastern Churches could not accept this and saw it as a diminution of the role of the Spirit, making him subordinate to the Son which alters the image of a Trinity of equal essential parts, a community in partnership. It was not only this rift which concerned the BCC, but the way that this had developed in recent times. They saw a western church divided between those who had almost no theology of Spirit and those who were much engaged with the Spirit as the agent of Christ in the world. Neither of these understandings can be truly Trinitarian.

The Third Person

For a Trinitarian theology to have integrity it is essential that there is a concrete and clearly discernible third person. Yet this is not always seen in the writing and the imagery of the church itself. Many of the images of the Trinity comprise two figures and a dove. This is particularly true of the western church and by the 16th century artists such as Duerer, Van Aelst and El Greco used this version of the image so widely that there can

---

[10] *The Forgotten Trinity*, The British Council of Churches, Inter-Church House, London, 1989

be little doubt as to the general conception from which they worked. Such imagery offers what can only be described as a duality, for the dove hovers above or ascends from the two figures in a way that suggests something borne forth from the two persons rather than an equal partner in a unity of three. Even Titian's "The Trinity in Glory" which does have three persons has the third person on a lower level, between the glory of the Father and the Son and humanity in supplication.

The early church fathers could speak powerfully about a belief in God and in his Son but tended to offer a much weaker case for their understanding of the Holy Spirit. The very weakness of their case, however, does suggest not a lack of belief, but a deficiency of explanation. Despite their limited explanation of the Third Person, the Holy Spirit is included as "the sanctifier of the faith of those who believe in the Father, and in the Son, and in the Holy Ghost."[11] The Spirit is the imbuer of holiness, even Jesus at his baptism has holiness conferred by the Spirit. This relationship offers an image of a being apart, not an emanation of Jesus himself, but sent by the Father. The action of sending infers a being other than so in that concept we are offered a third person.

The Second Person

In this usage we must be careful not to fall into the trap of thinking of Jesus of Nazareth as "The Second Person of the Trinity". This is the Logos, the Word of God, The Christ. There is of course, a considerable philosophical and linguistic

---

[11]Tertullian, *Against Praxeas*, chapter 12.

debate as to the correct understanding of "Logos", but the church has generally used it in the sense of "Word" and scholars and theologians have expressed this as an understanding of God's creative activity. Genesis tells us, in most English translations, "God said:" to preface each act of the creation of the world and the skies in which it was set. When Captain Picard in Star Trek Next Generation, issues a command with his catchphrase "Make it so!" this is a direct referencing of the Word of God.

In Matthew Chapter 8 verse 5 Jesus is approached by a centurion: 5When Jesus had entered Capernaum, a centurion came and pleaded with Him, 6"Lord, my servant lies at home, paralyzed and in terrible agony."

7"I will go and heal him," Jesus replied.

8The centurion answered, "Lord, I am not worthy to have You come under my roof. But just say the word, and my servant will be healed. 9For I myself am a man under authority, with soldiers under me. I tell one to go, and he goes; and another to come, and he comes. I tell my servant to do something, and he does it."

10When Jesus heard this, He marvelled and said to those following Him, "Truly I tell you, I have not found anyone in Israel with such great faith.

This passage is another example of a form of belief that we do not expect. The centurion does not only deal with Jesus as a bearer of authority but as someone who holds authority beyond the power of the earthly. Unlike those who are clamouring for him to come and do miracles, he simply accepts that the Word of Jesus will do what is needed.

Despite the conversation in Job, the ancients did not think of God as physically laying foundations and setting in place stones to create the earth, they were thinking of God, and God commands does not labour. So here we can see what is meant when Jesus is called the Word of God. John's gospel in its opening verse gives this concept life as it puts it in the context of the first Genesis story. "In the beginning was the Word, and the Word was with God, and the Word was God. He was with God in the beginning." John is identifying the Christ as the creator of all that was made. Notice that John says "all that was made". The Christ, the Son of God is not made, but is present in the beginning.

Irenaeus[12] describes God the *Father* as uncreated, uncontained, invisible, creator of the universe and the *Son of God* as the Word of God whose role was to restore fellowship between God and humanity. This is the central part of his economy[13] of creation. Within this economy he sees the role of the Holy Spirit as to be poured out on humanity as a renewal.

The Incarnation
In the Incarnation the Church claims that God came to earth, was made "man" in a child born to a woman and through this life has a new relationship with humanity. Jesus of Nazareth lived on earth as a human being, experiencing the emotions, troubles, joys and horrors of life amongst his creations. Variously it is claimed that in this man we can encounter a God we can relate to rather than the transcendent God encountered

---

[12] Demonstration of Apostolic Preaching

[13] Economy here is used as a reference to the interaction of God with his creation. God's salvation is offered by the action of the Word and brought to us by the Holy spirit.

by the Old Testament prophets; a God who has experienced our life; and this is the person of the Trinity whose role it is to restore humanity's relationship with God to that of perfection. To be clear it is not Jesus of Nazareth who brings restoration, it is the Son who is in him who does this. In Exodus 3:6 Moses meets God and "hid his face because he was afraid to look at him. Later, in Chapter 20:18-19 the people were so afraid of God that they pleaded that he should not speak to them or they would die. Elijah covered his face on the mountain when he went out to hear God speak. Isaiah too is terrified of God. Faced with a vision of the glory of the Lord his response is "Woe to me!" I cried. "I am ruined! For I am a man of unclean lips, and my eyes have seen the King, the Lord Almighty." all typical of the reaction of those who encountered God as described in the Old Testament. Their God was a fearsome and vengeful creature attested to by all the prophets as they told how God would deal with the Israelites for their disobedience and failures. Had the Israelites misunderstood God through all their history? In some ways it would seem that this was so. He forgave them, offered chance after chance and send a legion of prophets to persuade them to change their ways. But there was a difference in what is presented through Jesus of Nazareth. His teaching focuses on a forgiving and loving God who is seeking a relationship with all humanity. Of course it is not as simple as that. The sacrifice the gospels tell of is uncomfortable for many people and today many have a Universalist[14] bent which makes the statements regarding belief in Jesus and the possibility that not all will enter salvation objectionable to them.

---

[14] This understanding means that ALL will be saved. Not even Wesley makes that statement.

What the Bible presents us with in Matthew and Luke is a story of salvation. The child is created for the purpose of saving people from their sins. His life, his preaching and, in the end, his death are salvic in intent and this can be seen in all his preaching and his statements regarding his own end. Luke tells us he will be called "Son of God"[15], Matthew has the angel call him "Emmanuel which means 'God is with us'."[16] Only John makes a reference which can be interpreted as in any way Trinitarian. His references to the light to which he was to testify[17] relate directly to his opening discourse and identify Jesus, whom he points to later, as the Word of God. In verse fourteen he goes even further and tells us "the Word became flesh and lived among us", this is the only direct reference to incarnation in the Gospels just as his usage of "God the only Son"[18] can be a more direct pointer to a Trinitarian theology. All of these interpretations are capable of being disputed. Many biblical scholars will contest the English translation and offer a different context and will have some problem with the provenance of the Gospel of John in any case.

The reality is that the Church has maintained a belief in the Trinity as central to Christian faith since at least the fourth century. Ever since we have been embroiled in the question of what we mean when we speak of it.

---

[15]Luke 1:25.

[16]Matthew 1:23.

[17]John 1:6-11.

[18]John 1:14.

The Baptism

Each of the Gospels has this as an integral part. The three synoptic gospels use very much the same words, in particular in regard to the descent of the Holy Spirit and the words addressed to Jesus from heaven. "You are my Son, the Beloved". Most commentators are at pains to remind us that "Son of God" and "God's Son" are not specific to Jesus in biblical usage or indeed more generally throughout this period of history. It is in the reception of the Holy Spirit that Jesus's ministry is initiated. John's Gospel is specific in that the Baptist makes clear that he baptises with water and Jesus, who will follow, will baptise with the Holy Spirit.

Although Jesus himself did not baptise, his disciples did so, Baptising with water as John had done. The Holy Spirit came at Pentecost, as an adjunct to baptism, for it comes from God and when Peter and John joined Philip in Samaria it was they who laid on hands and offered the gift of the Holy Spirit. It would seem that what Jesus received at his baptism was being passed on by the apostles.

The Crucifixion

In each of the three synoptic gospels the story told is in most aspects the same. The onlookers and the soldiers mock him and demand that he save himself if he is the Christ. Only in Luke does Jesus cry out "Father into your hands I commit my spirit." But in all, his death is followed by the tearing apart of the curtain of the temple, which in Luke leads directly to the Centurion responding "Surely this was a righteous man". But only the words of Jesus to the condemned man telling him that he would be in paradise with him offer any suggestion of a divine person.

We have to return to the Garden of Gethsemane to find a context for the crucifixion. Three times Jesus asks his Father if this final sacrifice is necessary. Each time he comes back to the disciples and finds the answer. They have not been able to remain awake while he prayed.. It is not his Father who demands the sacrifice, it is the need to create a permanent act, that of death and resurrection to raise them from their slumber and create the elements of a permanent mission on the earth.

After the Third Day

Even after the resurrection the disciples have not got the message. Jesus appears first to the women at the tomb and they are sent to the disciples, but even then the disciples are in despair. It is not until Jesus appears amongst then in the upper room and at Emmaus that they began to wake up and we are taken, in Acts, to the upper room and the coming of the Holy Spirit first to the disciples and then after their preaching it being poured out on the great crowd at Pentecost.

CHAPTER FIVE

GOD IN RELATIONSHIP – THE SOCIAL TRINITY

It is sometimes suggested that the Trinity is God in a relationship, this is a tricky concept, but it is suggesting that the three "persons" of the trinity exist in relationship to each other. This concept leads to a possible differentiation of the three persons which takes away from the One God concept which is central to our understanding of God. Those theologians who are concerned in thinking about this idea also offer what they call a social trinity, prominent amongst these are Jürgen Moltmann, David Cunningham and Paul Fiddes.

For me the problem with this expression of Trinity is that it seems to slip away from the one God stance from which we start our creedal understanding of God. I struggle with some of the ways this is worked out when discussing the three persons of the Trinity, but more problematic for me is the ease with which they slip into the particular concept of a greater community. When we celebrate communion, we are absolutely celebrating being invited to communion with God, but not to be part of the community that is God, but that is where the social Trinitarians wander.

A much used word to describe this is *perichoresis* which literally means that one person contains the other in a static sense, or that one person interpenetrates another in the active sense the Greek Fathers understood this as a "perichoretic dance" which was their way of expressing three persons in one without losing the individual persons. Unfortunately Fiddes decided to illustrate the cover of his book on social trinity with a Matisse painting, called the dance. This seems to have given many writers to take this literally

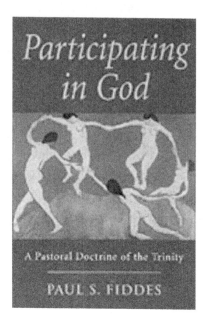

As you can see, there are five people in the dance in this illustration, and having that in mind, some have started to use the concept of Christians being part of the dance. That would suggest that we have become a part of the body of God, having interpenetrated the Trinity and become one with it.

Paul had great problems with a heretical group called Gnostics. Part of their belief was that we, humans, were a spark of light descended from the divine and that when we died we returned to the divine body. And this sounds awfully like the ideas the social Trinitarians are sliding into..

If had to find an illustration of the perichoretic dance I would not use a group dancing in a circle, but an eightsome reel! But it would still not illustrate a Trinitarian dance

Despite my difficulties with some of the uses made of social Trinitarian theology, it has a strong following and there are some of the ideas it espouses which it is important to be aware of.

One example of Social Trinitarian Theology

Paul Fiddes is a British Baptist theologian known for his contributions to the fields of theology, ethics, and Baptist studies. He has engaged with the concept of the social Trinity in his theological work, particularly emphasizing the communal and relational aspects within the Godhead. Fiddes has emphasized the idea of communion within the Trinity, underscoring the mutual relationships and love shared among the three persons—Father, Son, and Holy Spirit. His work reflects an interest in the social dimensions of God's existence. In Fiddes' theological exploration, there is an emphasis on the mutual sharing and giving within the Trinity. This focus aligns with the social Trinity perspective, which highlights the idea that the persons of the Trinity exist in a dynamic and reciprocal relationship of love. He extends the social Trinity concept into the life of the Christian community (ecclesiology). He explores how the communal nature of the Trinity serves as a model for understanding and shaping the relationships within the community of faith.

Another is offered through the lens of Liberation Theology

Leonardo Boff is a Brazilian theologian and former Franciscan friar and has made significant contributions to Liberation Theology and ecotheology. In his theological reflections, Boff engages with the concept of the social Trinity, aligning it with his broader concerns for social justice, ecological responsibility, and the liberation of marginalized communities. Boff, influenced by Liberation Theology, emphasizes the social and communal dimensions of the Trinity. He sees the divine community as a model for human community, emphasizing mutual relationships and interconnectedness he extends the social Trinity to address social and economic injustices.

Boff believes that the relationships within the Trinity should inspire Christians to work for a more just and equitable society, reflecting the inclusive and compassionate nature of God.

As you can see, both of these writers are very concerned with the community and the way Christians work in and with the community and relate their Trinitarian theology to societal needs and works. Thinking such as this offers many advantages when considering the way the church relates with the community around it.

CHAPTER SIX

FEMINIST TRINITARIAN THEOLOGY

The reality is that the words we use to describe God are based in an ancient culture. To the people of the early Bible man was the creator in the making of a child and woman was the bearer. This imagery, for them, mirrored the creation of the world, in that God the Father created the world and the universe birthed it. This patriarchal language and culture continued into the twentieth century in Britain, it was only 100 years ago, that women began to become free of male domination in almost all parts of society. But while women have been largely emancipated, we are still stuck with the semantic problem.

Theologically, Jesus is God's Son, and God is the Father, not only of Jesus, but of all creation. There would seem to be no reason why we could not speak of Mother God and her Daughter, except that simply turns the insult on its head. I have, for some time, used "children" when the text says "sons", but it is not an exact synonym

James Torrance wrote: "God is love. Love always implies communion between persons, and that is what we see supremely in God." While he went on to remind us that "God created man in his own image, in the image of God he created him: Male and female he created them (Gen 1:26-27)[19]

Yet having written a sterling support of gender equality, he could not find it possible to offer a gender neutral formula for the texts.

---

[19] Gender Sexuality and the Trinity, James Torrance, 1998

In the Old Testament, the sacred name for God *Jahweh* is gender neutral but has no usage in New Testament writings other than in the "I am" saying of Jesus in the Gospel of John. This usage is a reference to the episode in Exodus when Moses met God at the burning bush and God told him "tell them I am sent me". I am is an English translation of *Jahweh*,[20] since after this time the Israelites referred to God principally as Lord and we use the term still in worship and prayer, this may be less of an offence if we spoke of God as the Lord rather than father, but it has no usefulness in the Trinitarian nomenclature.

The bible contains a number of verses in which there are feminine images for God:

As a mother comforts her child,
so I will comfort you;
you shall be comforted in Jerusalem
(Is. 66:13).

Can a woman forget her nursing child,
or show no compassion for the child of her womb?
Even these may forget,
yet I will not forget you.
(Is. 49:15)
For a long time I have kept my peace,
I have kept still and restrained myself;
now I will cry out like a woman in labour,
I will gasp and pant.[21] Isaiah 42:14

---

[20] Exodus 3:14

[21] The Case for Women's Ministry, Ruth Edwards SPCK 133-43

The last of these verses is in fact the voice of God in the text.

These verses offer a wide and useful series of images of God in a feminine mode, but could be equally countered by the far more frequent masculine usages. Of course once we get into the New Testament, we are solely faced with male names and in the references to the partners in the Trinity nothing else.

I suspect that we may find that for all practical purposes, 'the masculine terminology of the New Testament will be with us as long as the New Testament is with us.'23

One usage that has gained some popularity with those seeking to find a more inclusive language is to use the formula Creator, Redeemer, Sustainer. This has some appeal and I know that there are number of ministers who use it, even in the blessing. The problem with this wording is that it tells us what God *does*, not who he *is*, in short it is a form of modalism.[22]

Some would argue that this inclusive language is more important than a fine point of definition of theological problem such as the Trinity. Jurgen Moltmann dealt with this problem and replied: "Dialogue with other religions is not helped if Christians relativize that which is distinctively Christian and give it up in favour of a general pluralism. Who would be interested in a dialogue with Christian theologians who no longer want to advocate Christianity clearly.[23]" Simply put, if it doesn't matter to us what we believe, we are no longer living as people of faith.

---

[22] Modalism refers to the separating the "persons" of God by the things they do. This separates them and infers that each has a purpose on its own.

[23] Jurgen Moltmann, Trans. John Bowden, *History and the Triune God*, SCM Press, London

This essay is an attempt to describe what the Church and our history means when they talk of the Trinity. In no way do I mean to say that if you do not understand it fully, you are not Christian, what I am saying is that if you deny the Trinity in the understanding of one God In three Persons and look to explain God in a different way, you are moving away from our beliefs. As you can see throughout this work, the greatest minds of the Church for centuries have struggled to state this element of the Christian faith but the struggle should not lead to denial.

Karl Barth, the Swiss theologian, one of the most influential of the early twentieth century held revelation as a central doctrine of the Christian theologian and preacher. By this he meant that God was revealed to us in the scriptures. In the scriptures God sends his Son to be our redeemer, and

God is sometimes spoken of in the Old Testament as Father of the people, or a God who will look after Israel as would a father, but Jesus reveals God as His Father, in a direct relational way, not as a synonym as he does with his use of Son. It is through Jesus, the Son, that God is revealed to us in Trinity.

Although in the very opening of the book of Genesis we are told how the Spirit moved over the waters it is the Son who tells us that God will send the Spirit to us as a counsellor and helper.

Printed in Great Britain
by Amazon

42452256R00030